1 MONTH OF
FREE
READING

at
www.ForgottenBooks.com

By purchasing this book you are eligible for one month membership to ForgottenBooks.com, giving you unlimited access to our entire collection of over 1,000,000 titles via our web site and mobile apps.

To claim your free month visit:
www.forgottenbooks.com/free152299

ISBN 978-0-483-69636-5
PIBN 10152299

This book is a reproduction of an important historical work. Forgotten Books uses state-of-the-art technology to digitally reconstruct the work, preserving the original format whilst repairing imperfections present in the aged copy. In rare cases, an imperfection in the original, such as a blemish or missing page, may be replicated in our edition. We do, however, repair the vast majority of imperfections successfully; any imperfections that remain are intentionally left to preserve the state of such historical works.

THE VOICE

OF

OUR BROTHER'S BLOOD:

ITS SOURCE AND ITS SUMMONS.

A DISCOURSE

OCCASIONED BY THE SUMNER AND KANSAS OUTRAGES.

Preached in Newark, June 8th and 15th, 1856.

BY HENRY C. FISH,

PASTOR OF THE FIRST BAPTIST CHURCH.

NEWARK, N. J.,
DOUGLASS & STARBUCK, PRINTERS AND PUBLISHERS,
123 Market Street.

NEWARK, JUNE 30TH, 1856.
REV. AND DEAR SIR—

We, the undersigned, take occasion to express to you our very great satisfaction with the sentiments expressed in your recent discourse upon the existing difficulties that afflict us as a Nation, and the means of their removal. Believing that such views should have the widest possible circulation, we respectfully request a copy of the discourse for publication.

With sentiments of high esteem and regard, we remain,

Yours, truly,

HORACE J. POINTER,	THEO. P. HOWELL,	S. G. GOULD,
JOSEPH C. HORNBLOWER,	PETER MEAD,	D. M. WILSON,
WILLIAM PENNINGTON,	THOMAS LAFON,	T. V. JOHNSON,
ASA WHITEHEAD,	WILLIAM SILVEY,	WILLIAM NORRIS,
DAVID A. HAYES,	Z. H. KITCHEN,	B. C. MILLER,
NEHEMIAH PERRY,	O. THAYER,	JOSEPH C. BATTIN,
MATTHIAS W. DAY,	J. W. STOUT, JR.,	D. C. RUNYON.

To the Rev. H. C. FISH, Newark, N. J.

———————

To the Honorable HORACE J. POINTER, Mayor of the City of Newark, Ex-Chief Justice JOSEPH C. HORNBLOWER, Ex-Gov. WILLIAM PENNINGTON, ASA WHITEHEAD, Esq., DAVID A. HAYES, Esq., NEHEMIAH PERRY, Esq., and others:

GENTLEMEN—It affords me pleasure to know that the sentiments of the discourse referred to in your note of yesterday, meet with approval. Although uttered with no expectation of publicity beyond the limits of a single congregation, yet I see no good reason for declining to comply with your kind request that they may have a wider circulation. A copy of the discourse is therefore placed at your disposal.

Indulging the hope that your interest in this regard may promote the best of causes,

I am, with sincere respect,

Yours, &c.,

HENRY C. FISH.

NEWARK, July 1st, 1856.

THE VOICE OF OUR BROTHER'S BLOOD.

" The voice of thy brother's blood crieth unto me from the ground."
—GEN. 4 : 10.

We have come up hither to meditate upon grave concerns. We have come out of love to our country's interests. There is commotion in the land. There is violence and blood. A brother has been stricken down. The blow was not a private injury. It was a public wrong. It smote the body of this great Commonwealth. It smote it at a vital point. There is no other point *so* vital. The Senate Chamber is the inner sanctuary of our liberties. It is the place where the weightiest affairs of the Republic are to be seriously, wisely, dispassionately, and fearlessly debated, and considered, and decided. Rome lost her liberties by suffering encroachment on the Senate ; and had not the revolution restored to England the equilibrium of her government, she, too, had lost hers from the same cause. Infringe upon the freedom and integrity of the Senate, and you have smitten the heart of these Sovereign States. The blow, then, that fell our brother, was, intentionally or otherwsie, a blow at the most sacred interests of this whole nation.

Nor was it from a sudden outburst of passion. It was cool, calculated, deliberate :—more than this, it was the result of a malicious combination. The colleague of the wounded man has termed it an *assault.* This were a sufficient wrong ; but there is the best reason for believing that the act was rather a *conspiracy* than an *assault.* Nor is it by any means certain that it was not murderous in its design, as, in fact, it may yet prove to have been in execution. What is worse than all, the outrage is espoused by most of those in sympathy with the cowardly assassin who committed it. By some it is dignified with the name of *patriotism.* Others term it *just, noble, brave, heroic.* Testimonials are presented to the "chivalrous" Representative, for his " well-directed " services ; and his constituents are called together cordially to endorse, by a series of resolutions, the conduct of their "gallant countryman ;" while a leading Southern journal declares the act " good in conception, better in execution, and best of all in consequence ;" and concludes by saying, " We trust other gentlemen will follow the example, that so a curb may be imposed upon the truculence and audacity of abolition speakers. If need be, let us have a caning or cowhiding every day. If the worse come to the worse, so much the sooner so much the better."

In view of such facts, who can doubt that this barbarous attack upon a Northern Senator is but the inauguration of the *code of blood*, and of the reign of *brute force*? Indeed, it was before this inaugurated. For months past it has reigned at the Capitol. In December last, the editor of the *Evening Star* was assaulted and beaten in the lobby of the House, by a Representative from Virginia. Then the editor of a New York journal was assailed with blows in the grounds of the Capitol, by a member from Arkansas. Then another hot-blood from the South shot down and killed an Irish waiter at a hotel. And now, a gentleman, noted for his lettered acquirements and Senatorial dignity and propriety, is knocked down senseless upon the very floor of the Senate Chamber, and in his own chair, for nothing save the legitimate discharge of his sworn obligations.

All this is significant. Freedom of speech is to be suppressed. Every one knows that it is now suppressed to a great extent in the South. The same is almost equally true at Washington. It is becoming unsafe there to utter a word against the "peculiar institution." Threats and abuses have proved unavailing, and henceforth the friends of freedom and humanity are to be met with pistols and dirks, and bludgeons. To use the words of a journal, already referred to, (the *Richmond Enquirer*,) the "pack of curs" must "be *lashed* into submission." "Let them once understand, that for every vile word spoken against the South, they will suffer so many *stripes*, and they will soon learn to behave themselves like *decent dogs !*" And this is the language—not of Austria or Rome—but of free America! Alas l where is our freedom, when free men cannot speak—no, not even within those walls once consecrated, in the eyes of envious nations, to the cause of Freedom, but now, most sad to tell, desecrated by freemen's blood !

But the Capitol is not the *only* scene of violence and blood.

Just yonder, midway between Virginia and California, and Minnesota and Texas,—and hence almost in the exact natural center of the United States—do I witness scenes at which the heart sickens, and every feeling of humanity revolts. That beautiful land, with an unused soil of surpassing richness, and a well-tempered climate, inviting the invalid and giving strength to the strong—a land every way to be desired—is the scene of desolation, and cruelty, and death. All over those broad green prairies, roam unhung murderers, with hands and lips red with blood, and breathing forth against unoffending victims, fire and slaughter. Now they trample down the fields seeded with grain ; now they kill the domestic animals of free-State men, which come in their way ; now they burn their hay-ricks and steal or destroy the implements of husbandry ; now they seize a preacher of the gospel, and tie him to a log and throw him into the river ; now they shoot a man at work in his field ; now they break open the doors of quiet habitations, commit barbarities upon the women and children, and steal and devour with the zest of infuriated fiends. And now they seek some provocation as a cover for seizing upon a free-State settlement, setting fire to its houses, blowing up its public buildings, casting its printing presses into the streams, and expelling, with armed force, those inoffensive citizens whose bones are not left in the ashes of the smouldering ruins. And now they seize upon every friend of freedom—even those with Congressional authority—and some they imprison, and some they cut with knives and hatchets, and some they brutally kill.

Is the Lord unmindful of all these things ? I tell you nay ! His ear is open to the cry of the oppressed. There is a voice in the blood of those who suffer unrighteously. That of Abel, in our text, reached the ear of the Eternal. The moist and reddened ground uttered its mute accents, and called for vengeance upon the offender. So is there a voice in the blood that now stains the halls of our Legislation, and fattens the soil of our western prairies. God hears it ; man hears it ; and we have come together to ponder it well.

I ask two things : *why* the shedding of this blood ; and *to what* it calls us.

I. THE SOURCE.

And here, as well as throughout this discourse, I shall speak freely and plainly. I belong to no party, or society ; I speak for no party; and I have no personal ends to gain. I speak as the friend of humanity. I speak from the stand-point of gospel truth. I speak to protect and advance the interests of my country, with all her sacred institutions, and by so doing promote the welfare of a fallen world.

What, then, I again ask, is the *source* of all these existing difficulties ? It is easily told ; and I will open the whole matter in few words. *It is the resurrection of the Slave Power, and the indifference or subserviency of the people of the Free States to that power.*

There was a time when the slave interests of this country were not widely operative. Viewed in the light of an inherited institution, in itself an *evil*, but not easily disposed of, the men of even one generation ago, said and cared but comparatively little as to its perpetuity or extension.

About the time indicated, however, that is about the year 1820, the Slave Power experienced a wonderful resurrection. To borrow a figure, it was at the Ithuriel touch of the Missouri discussion (then before Congress,) that slavery started up, portentous and swollen with rage, and loud with threats and assumptions. Some attribute this resuscitation to the excesses of Northern abolitionists. I would be far from endorsing all that has been said and done at the North against slavery; but to attribute to *this* the revival of the Slave Power were simply idle and ridiculous. It is often *asserted*, but is too absurd to be disproved. It was the heat engendered in the discussion as to whether Missouri should be admitted as a slave State, that sent new life into the slave system. Many of the great statesmen of that day believed that the Constitution did not recognize slavery ; or, at the most, viewed it as a *local* institution, to be protected where it was planted, but not to be extended beyond existing limits. It was decided, however, as a final compromise, that Missouri should be admitted, but that slavery should be prohibited in all the remaining territory west of the Mississippi, and north of 36 degrees and 30 minutes, leaving entirely untouched by the arrangement all lands south of this line, or subsequently to be acquired. This solemn covenant, or compact, was called a compromise, and was adopted at the urgent solicitations of slaveholders and those in their interests, *as the condition of admitting the new State into the Union*. Without this condition, that State would not have been admitted. And its adoption was looked upon by the upholders of slavery, to use the words of a distinguished South Carolinian, written on the night of the passage of the Compromise, as "*a great triumph ;*" while multitudes at the north were humbled, and grieved, and afflicted.

But mark the course of opinions and events. Since that time, the sentiment of the South, as regards slavery, has undergone a wonderful revolution. Within a few years, it has been held up by its defenders, as a blessing instead of a curse ; a system founded in the nature of things, elevating in its tendency, and absolutely indispensable as an American institution. What the fathers regarded as an evil to be endured for a time, the sons are regarding as a positive good, to be nurtured and perpetuated. And to perpetuate it, and render it profitable, like every thing else, it must have scope and control. The *people* may care little for its extension, but the *politicians* will not hold the balance of power and enjoy *national patronage* and *preferment* without it. "If the newly acquired territory be carved up into free States, the north, and not the south, will elect the governmental officers, and have everything their own way."

Thus reasoned those whose trade was politics, or whose peenniary interest, and honor, and popularity were identified with the barbarous system in question. And reasoning thus, every energy has of late been bent in that direction. The odious Fugitive Slave Bill was an outgrowth of this new life in the Slave Power. So was the gradual instalment in places of trust and power, of men in sympathy with this interest, until it is not without reason apprehended, that the highest tribunal in the land could not be brought to give a decision unfavorable to the slave interest. Nay, in view of a possible, (perhaps *probable*,) decision of the Supreme Court, to the effect that slaves may be held, by authority of the Constitution, while being transported through the free States, (and, of course, if held by its authority in free States *one hour*, they may be *one year*, or *any* term of years,) in view, I say, of the possibility of such a decision, men at the South are making their boast that they will yet call the roll of their bondmen on Bunker Hill itself !

But the most astonishing and humiliating illustration of the revival of the Slave Power, is found in the famous Kansas-Nebraska Act. By this Act, the solemn covenant of compromise, above referred to, was violated and rescinded. It was a deep plot, laid in the guile and craft of the devil himself, steeped and concocted in perjury, hypocrisy and black injustice, and basely sprung upon the people, through the treacherousness of their leaders, before they had the opportunity to express their will, or put forth their legitimate power. Thus was the old landmark of Freedom overturned, and the new territory opened to the introduction of the monster slavery.

Still, the question was professedly to be left to the settlers of the new territory, whether slavery should or should not exist within its limits. But observe the results. First of all, the Governor, Secretary, Chief Justice, other Justices and the Attorney or Marshal, were not elected by the people of the territory, but sent from Washington, and were supposed to be in the interest of the dominant party, and consequently to shape everything in that direction. Next, the first election of a delegate to Congress was to take place. Let the tale be told in a single sentence. Hordes of reckless invaders crossed the line, and came into Kansas in the guise of voters, and stole away the right of the people to decide the choice for themselves. Next, the Territorial Legislature was to be elected ; when an armed multitude, with tents and organized companies, and munitions, and beating drums, and streaming flags, entered the territory, and everywhere exercised the complete control of the election, and thus imposed upon the people a Legislature repulsive to their will. Again, in October last, at the choice of a member for Congress, the same invasion, and the same forced election are well known matters of history. And a like external force was employed at the adoption of the Constitution, in December last.

The recent sacking of the town of Lawrence, and the unbounded control of armed desperadoes, complete the last scene in this history of usurpation and crime yet opened to our view.

Thus has the Slave Interest, impelled by an unwonted lust for extension and control, been grasping within its deadly embraces, the places of honor and trust, and the fair portions of the land, once dedicated to Justice, and Freedom, and Righteousness.

And here lies the secret of our present National afflictions. The champions of oppression have become bold and rampant. They will not brook restraint. Reckless as to the *means*, they are bound to compass, *somehow*, their ambitious ends. If fair means will not answer, foul means must. And woe to him who places a straw in their way! If a man be found in Kansas, with the taint of northern principles, he must be got rid of somehow—either by intimidation, or abuse, or by the bowie knife and revolver. If witnesses are brought before a Commission, to testify to unfair proceedings, they must be arrested for high treason and ordered to leave the territory, or locked up in prison. And if a man, even at Washington, dare to express, with frankness, his views of the injustice of these proceedings, he must be cudgeled into silence !

But I said the source of this violence and bloodshed was the resurrection of the Slave Power, *and the indifference or subserviency of northern men to this power.*

I wish to utter a few words on this last point—the conduct of men at the North. The South is not wholly responsible for the calamities under review. A large share of the responsibility rests on the people of these free States. To the eternal disgrace of these States, it must be said, that the ostensible originator of the Bill repealing the Missouri Compromise, was a man from a free State !

And it is a fact not less humiliating, that the Chief Executive,

who has so ingloriously figured as a willing tool in these transactions,
was reared on the free hills of New England ! I would not speak
evil of the ruler of the people, although I discard the sentiment
that the voice of the ruler is necessarily the voice of God; and insist
that his conduct, like all other officials, should be closely scrutinized,
and if need be condemned. A ruler is entitled to my respect just so
far as he rules righteously, and not one whit farther. But as respects
the *line of conduct* pursued by the National Executive, I hold it
up to universal detestation. Quick to scent the savor of rebel-
lion at the north, wherever the good people resisted the at-
tempts of slave hunters to catch the poor fugitives who claimed their
God-given rights—quick to invent strange means whereby to secure
to a southern slaveholder an item of his alleged property, caught in
the streets of Boston, and to say to the U. S. Attorney at Boston,
"Incur any expense deemed necessary to insure the execution of the
law," he can see an honored Senator, from that same city, knocked
down and well nigh killed, in defiance of God's laws and man's, and
neither utter one word of disfavor, nor perform the part of a friend
by calling to see whether he be dead or alive ! If a slave breeder
chance to require it, thousands of dollars of the public funds are
expended in bringing back an escaped mulatto; but when, in one of
the provinces placed under his protection, hundreds of women and
children are sent shrieking from their homes—when white men, simply for their free principles, are waylaid, and shot down, and hunted
like the partridge on the mountain—when the ballot-box is polluted
and rifled, and the most sacred right of a free citizen—his elective
franchise—is set at defiance, *then* he folds his hands, and looks coolly
on, and deems he has no power to redress the wrongs !

Nay, what is infinitely worse, he absolutely turns oppressor himself,
by enforcing the doings of a legislature which every man knows to
have been a sham and a farce. The President himself knows it and
admits it, though reluctantly, in declaring the creative transactions
to have been "*illegal* and *reprehensible!*" And yet the *acts* of this
so-called legislature, he *is now supporting and enforcing* by United
States troops ; and by border ruffians scooped together, and placed
under command, and *paid out of the public treasury!* Alas ! how
do ambition and lust for power, and love of honor, blunt the moral
sense and lead one to repudiate his humanity, and become the mere
paw of mousing demagogues and fawning sycophants !

And I would that the President *alone* were liable to this impu-
tation. The truth is, there are *white* slaves as well as black, in

the District of Columbia, aye, and at the North, too. There are there and here, "Northern men with Southern principles," who would not say their souls were their own, if it were to offend slaveholders, or lose caste with the powers that be.

It is enough to make the blood of a true patriot tingle to his fingers' ends, to behold the indifference and subserviency of even liberty-loving men to the aggressions of the Slave Power. Some are so wedded to party interests as to have disfranchised themselves, and lost every particle of their political independence. But more are timid and time-serving from their social and business relations. They have friends and patrons in the southern States. The profits of their *trade* are drawn from that direction. To speak a word *against* slave propagandism might offend "a customer." To be found in the ranks of "Northern abolitionists," or to be known as advocating free sentiments, or acting in their support, might seriously affect their *income!* And hence, if they do not actually join in the cry, " Great is Diana of the Ephesians," they are sure to be found advising *extreme caution;* or secretly whispering, *" This our craft is in danger, and ye know that by this craft we have our wealth !"**

Why, therefore, should *not* oppressors become proud and insolent, when even the *Sons of the Pilgrims* have either sold themselves to their interests, or have lost the moral courage to sustain free principles, or speak forth boldly and openly in their support ? I ask, is it strange that usurpation and violence predominate, and their victims send up the cry for redress into the ear of the Almighty ?

Thus much as to the *Source.*

II. Let us now attend to the SUMMONS.

1. And first, the voice of our brother's blood calls to the exercise of *sympathy* and *brotherly concern.* We may not say, "Am I my brother's keeper ?" We are linked together, bone of the same bone, and flesh of the same flesh—the members of one common family. We are to weep with those that weep, and when one of our fellows suffers, we ought ourselves to feel afflicted ; thus bearing each other's burdens, and so fulfilling the law. When, therefore, the lovers of freedom in the halls of Congress, or in a distant territory, are shedding their blood in defence of the very liberties for which our fathers fought, and bled, and died, shall we deny them the hand of affection and the warm sympathies of our hearts ? Let us make their case our own. If *you* were the victim of assassination, now suffering from

---

* How striking a verification of the words of JOHN RANDOLPH, uttered many years ago:—
" *We govern you by your white slaves.*"

cruel wounds, or if *your* dearest rights, and your property, and your families, were outraged by hordes of drunken and maddened ruffians, would not indifference seem to you the veriest cruelty? It is well that the noble champion of humanity at Washington is receiving expressions of condolence and kindly encouragement. It were better if there were one general effort, on the part of the inhabitants of every town and village, to send to our suffering brethren in Kansas, the *substantial* proofs of our commisseration, and the words of sympathy and cheer, which they so much require.

2. The sad events to which I refer, summon us to *united* and *earnest prayer*. These are not the *only* threatening aspects upon our social and political horizon. The clouds lower and thicken in every direction. In one way or another, our government is on unpleasant terms with half the powers of Europe. Men at the South are mad upon their idols, and seem determined to install them, not only in our National Temples, but in the very homes of free men who love liberty better than life. And in this nefarious movement, they have the aid and sympathy of the Chief Executive, and of Congressmen not a few. Add to this the civil war now actually raging, with its horrid train of fire and slaughter, in our frontier settlements, and the unrebuked reign of daring violence at the Capitol, and one cannot but fear that God Almighty, in His just indignation for the wrongs and sins of this people, so long committed, is about to allow us to be precipitated into one general ruin; and to witness the vision of the prophet, "The battle of the warrior, with confused noise, and garments rolled in blood, and burning, and fuel of fire!" This seems plain, that we are either going fast to destruction, or that God is preparing some strange deliverance that shall glorify His providence and His great name.

Is not *such* a time a time for *prayer*? We have placed dependence in men and have been deceived. We have looked everywhere for deliverance and it has not come. Now let Israel say, "Our help is in the Lord God Almighty, that made the heavens and the earth!" Now let the saints of the Most High, *look unto the hills whence cometh their salvation!* Let the ministers in the courts of the Lord's house; let the parents at the family altar, and the people in their social gatherings, and the pious ones in the retirement of their closets—let the young and the old, the rich and the poor, the fathers and the mothers, the sons and the daughters—pour out their supplications before God, that He would thwart the plans of the oppressors, and open up a way of escape through the Red Sea of difficulty that now lies before us!

3. Finally, the voice of our brother's blood summons us to *action.*. Prayer and action go together. The Almighty never does that for us which we may do for ourselves. Words alone, and prayer alone, when we are *able to act*, are mere mockery. As faith without works is dead, so is prayer. " Heaven helps those who help themselves." There should be *action*, then. And that action should have a distinct and definite direction. It should aim to compass at least three things.

1. *The extinction of a rising despotism.*

Absolute power, unlimited by men, or constitution, or laws, is despotism. We have it not in *form*, but it is fearfully obtaining in *fact.*. New and strange constructions, to suit political purposes, are put by our rulers upon the laws of. the Commonwealth, and every year there is less and less regard for the popular opinion, so long as partizan ends are secured. The government is fast passing out of the hands of the people, into the hands of officials. Men put in office to do the public will—the *servants* of the free people who choose them—are coming to think that the seat of power is *in them*, and *not* in the *people ;* that they are to *govern*, and the people are *to be governed ;* that the will of their constituents is nothing, so long as they have the power to do their *own will ;* and hence, as often as it serves their purpose, they fearlessly override the known wishes of the majority of the sovereign people.

The tendency of any form of government is either to anarchy, where there is no law, or to an oligarchy, where the many are ruled by the few. The Republican government—the type which our fathers adopted —aims to secure the just medium between the two extremes of anarchy and despotism. But there is no surer way to induce anarchy than by encroaching on the rights of the people, and enacting laws *known to be contrary to their will.* No free people will long endure this. Now, of this nature, I hesitate not to say, was the *Fugitive Slave Bill ;* and, more particularly, the *Kansas-Nebraska Act.* The majority of the people of the United States were opposed to these acts. Had they not been adopted *as they were*—had the people had an opportunity to control the matter, by their popular elections— neither of those acts would have been adopted. As it was, they were precipitated upon the people, and that too in known violation of the prevailing sentiment. And they were but the cropping forth of an undergrowth of tyranny and oppression, which threatens the very existence of our glorious Union. The hydra-headed monster— Slavery—in the person of its champions and abettors, is setting at.

defiance all law and order, and the public sentiment of the North, and introducing a reign of despotism and brute violence, almost without a parallel among civilized nations.

If any one doubt it, let him look at still other indications. Let him look at the *attacks now made upon* FREE SPEECH. Freedom of speech is the very breath of a Republic. It is absolutely *essential* to liberty. When public doings are freely criticised by the press, and the pulpit, and the individual, there is little danger of the fruits of error. Only let the battle of Thought go on, and truth and right are sure to prevail. But when any public man, or any set of men, claim immunity from the closest scrutiny, and the freest possible criticism, and, if need be, censure; when free speech is killed to save public men, *then*, in the language of Milton, there is "a kind of massacre, whereof the extinction ends not in the slaying of an elemental life, but strikes at the etherial and fifth essence, *the breath of reason itself*, slaying an *immortality* rather than a life." As sings the Greek poet, Euripides :

> This is true liberty, when freeborn men,
> Having to advise the public, *may speak free;*
> Which he who can and will, deserves high praise;
> Who neither can, nor will, may hold his peace :
> What can be juster in a State than this?

But *are* we in the enjoyment of this right?—we, the free people of this Republic. I blush to tell the truth ! Every one knows, that while a man from the South may come North and speak with perfect freedom, of any one of our institutions, a man travelling at the South, or even residing there, and speaking freely against slavery, would be not less liable to lose his life than would a sojourner in Rome, if he made bold to traduce the Pope ; or a peasant in France or Russia if he dared to utter a word against the Emperor or the Czar.

The events of the past few months show how much freedom of speech there is on the common ground of the National Capitol. The outrage on Sumner was in open defiance of the Constitution itself. That instrument, wisely guarding the right of free speech in Congress, declares that "For any speech or debate in either House, they (the members,) shall not be called in question in any other place." Yet here is an instance of its open violation, (and by no means the first,) and its general sanction at the South makes it *representative* and fearfully significant. What must be the state of things, when for the expression of their opinions, members of Congress must carry deadly weapons as a means of defending life ! And then behold the so-called "laws" adopted by the pretended legislature of Kansas, and now in force in that ill-fated territory. In three sections only, there are no less than *forty-eight* denunciations of the penalty of *death,* by as many changes of language, for interfering with property in human flesh ! And *any one who denies, either by spoken or written word, " the right of persons to hold slaves in this territory," is denounced as a felon, and punishable by imprisonment at hard labor for a term not less than two years.* Even the PRESS, that object of universal dread to tyrants, as well as the tongue, is shackled and placed under a keen censorship. Hear the law, and say if it would not befit the veriest despot in the old world :

"SEC. 12. If any free person, by speaking or writing, assert or maintain that persons have not the right to hold slaves in this territory, or shall introduce into this territory, print, publish, write, circulate, or cause to be introduced in this territory, written, printed, published, or circulated in this territory, any book, paper, magazine, pamphlet or circular, containing any denial of the right of persons to hold slaves in this territory, such person shall be deemed guilty of felony, and punished by imprisonment at hard labor for a term of not less than two years."

Behold, then, our boasted freedom of speech ! Behold the encroachments of the Slave Power, made upon it, in the South, at the Capitol, and in the newly opened territory !*

---

* It was enactments like this, well termed the "DANCE of DEATH," that called forth, in the House of Representatives, those words of true eloquence from Mr. BINGHAM, of Ohio:

" Aye, sir, Congress is to abide by this statute which makes it a felony for a citizen to utter or publish in that Territory *'any thing calculated to* induce slaves to escape from the service of their masters.' Hence it would be felony there to utter the strong words of Algernon Sydney—'Resistance to tyrants is obedience to God;' a felony, to say with Jefferson, 'I have sworn upon the altar of my God eternal hostility to tyranny in every form over the mind and body of man ;' a felony to utter there in the hearing of a slave upon American soil, beneath the American flag, the words of flame which shook the stormy soul of Henry, 'Give me liberty, or give me death ;' a felony to read in the hearing of one of these fettered bondsmen the words of the Declaration, 'All men are born free and equal, and endowed by the Creator with the inalienable rights of life and liberty ;' a felony to utter those other words, blazing in letters of living light on the great written character of our National Government, ' We the people of the United States, in order to establish justice,' the attribute of God, and ' to secure liberty,' the imperishable right of man, do ' ordain this Constitution ;' a felony to harbor or aid a slave escaping from his thraldom ; a felony to aid freedom in its flight ; a felony to shelter the houseless, to clothe the naked, to feed the hungry, and to help him who is ready to perish ; a felony to give to the famishing a cup of water in the name of our Master. Oh, sir, before you hold this enactment binding on an American Congress, tear down the banner of freedom which floats above us, for stirring reminiscences linger in its folds, and the stars upon its field of azure have gleamed upon the field of 'poised battle,' where the earthquake and the fire led the charge, and where American virtue and American valor maintained the unequal conflict against the mighty power of British tyranny and oppression. Before you hold this enactment to be law, burn our immortal Declaration and our free-written Constitution, fetter our free press and finally penetrate the human soul, and put out the light of understanding which the breath of the Almighty hath kindled !"

Now, since this condition of national affairs is either originated or sanctioned and sustained by the majority of those who fill the high places of the land, I submit *that despotism is already installed over us!* I submit that there must be either *reformation* or *revolution!* I submit that the question as to the oppression of the colored race, has grown to the question of *the oppression of the free men of the north!* The issue before the people now is, *not* as to whether *negro* slavery shall exist, but whether *white* slavery shall be *endured!* In other words, the issue is, *Freedom* or *Despotism!*

And let the people *meet* this question! Full long enough have we been listless as to this great issue! We have remained quiet while the chains have been forging for our passive necks; if we remain indifferent and inactive *now, we deserve to wear them!*

2. As a second thing which present action should aim to compass, I mention *the arrest of the extension of slave territory.* I say the *arrest* of this extension, because its extension is already commenced, and out of it springs the present agitation. I thank high Heaven that there is yet left enough of virtue and moral courage, and Christian principle, to *resist* this monstrous wrong!

It is not of the *abolition* of slavery in the Southern States that I speak. I have purposely avoided the whole of this vexed question. I speak *only* of its *extension* into newly acquired territories. The original policy of this government, as all must concede, was Freedom and not Slavery. According to that policy, the question of slavery was a question with which the sovereign States choosing to sustain it were alone concerned. It was their own institution, with which the other States were not to interfere; but which was, in no sense whatever, a *national* institution. No provision whatever was made for its extension, nor even for its permission, on common territory. It was a thing not contemplated, and therefore wholly unprovided for. Slavery *was sectional* and not *national.* With it the nation, as such, had nothing to do. To disturb the original limitations, therefore, and attempt to *nationalize* slavery, is nothing less than breaking up the original foundations. Of right, no new slave states ought to have been created. Of right, the concessions of the Compromise in 1820, ought not to have been granted. They were granted solely for peace's sake.

And now to repeal that Compromise, and make the Constitution an instrument to carry slavery into free territory and shield it there with Executive authority, is a stupendous wrong against the people of the free States, and a rank offense before a just and holy God!

In His own Word was it written, of old, *"Cursed be he that removeth his neighbor's landmark;"* and all the people were to say, *"Amen!"* Was ever a landmark more sacred than that which set bounds to the aggressions of human servitude, and said hitherto mayest thou come *and no farther?* At least let *this* limitation be respected! Full enough have we already suffered from its unrighteous removal! And I do verily believe that it is but the first bitter dregs of that fearful cup which the Almighty will wring out unto us, if these aggressions continue!

To avert such a calamity, let every man stand to the right, and appeal to God against the oppressors! Let the voice of indignant remonstrance and the rally-cry of Freedom resound throughout the land! Let those who stand on Zion's walls set to the mouth the trumpet, and summon the people to the recovery of their departing liberties! Let the statesman from the hall of legislation, the jurist from his bench of justice, the lawyer from his office, the editor from his chair, the mechanic from his shop, and the husbandman from his fields, lift up the voice of united and earnest demand, and insist that *not one inch more* of the national domain be doomed to the blight and curse of human chattelship!

3. The remaining point to be gained, as the result of action imperatively demanded, is *purity and high moral principle in the men who administer our national affairs.* With some honorable exceptions, those who have of late held in their hands, so far as men may do it, the destinies of this nation, have given sad evidence of the want of these qualities. Time was when they were the chief characteristics of those who shared the people's honors. But in our day, politics has become too exclusively the trade of scoundrels. Government, for some time past, has been *manufactured by machinery*, and that machinery has been seized and worked by unscrupulous and venal aspirants. The future historian of our country will style this the *era of demagogueism.* This is the day when men of small mental caliber, and still smaller moral and virtuous capacities, figure in the high places, and from the power of their position are endangering the very existence of the Republic.

Who that looks upon the portraitures of the noble and venerable men who composed the first Congress of our country—the flower and pride of the land—and compares that group with those who fill the halls of Congress now, does not sicken at the disparity, and almost pray for the return of those lofty spirits, to shed light upon iour councils and lustre upon our age, and to lead us forth from our impending calamities?

But we need not wish them back. There are men among us not unworthy of their honored sires. All that is requisite is that we pull down from his position every office-bearer who has proved himself incompetent or recreant to his trust, and place in his stead a man who shall fear God and work righteousness. Men should now be called forth whose principles are known, and who can be *relied upon* —men who will be *statesmen,* as distinguished from *politicians ;* and who, at the behest of stern duty, are willing to stand the fight and endure the odium incurred *in doing right.* These are the men for the times. And to aid in calling them forth should be regarded as the sacred duty of every lover of his race.

Let not *Christian* men, especially, be indifferent to it. The fault, after all, lies with the people, who allow unprincipled men to usurp the places of trust. Disgusted with prevailing intrigue and corruption, good men have refrained from the exercise of their elective franchise. This is every way unwise; it is *more,* it is sinful in the sight of God. I have social and political duties, as well as duties strictly religious. It is not less my duty to render unto Cæsar the things that be Cæsar's, than unto God the things that be God's. Indeed, social and political duties *are* religious duties. Can it be shown where they do not interlace and interlap ? The truth is, religion should pervade every department of human life. It is not a thing to be put on and worn at certain seasons, and cast off again at convenience. It must be carried *everywhere.* A man should make it a matter of *conscience* to go to the polls : and he should go there just as he goes to church, or addresses himself to any duty—for the sole purpose of glorifying God. If the political atmosphere has become too corrupt for Christians to enter it, then let it be purified. So much the more need of the salt of their holy example and influence. Who has given authority to sunder religion from politics ? Where is the bill of divorcement ? The fruits of such an unnatural disseverance are already too patent. It is high time that an end be put to the producing cause.

We *pray* for our country's welfare ; but we are to pray for nothing which we are not ready to secure or promote, so far as in us lies. It is the grossest inconsistency for a man to bow at the altar of prayer in his family, and ask for good rulers, and then refuse to do his part to secure them.

And let me say in conclusion, that in the effort to secure the several ends indicated in this discourse, there ought to be an universal and harmonious endeavor.

I think I have set forth what is the real seat of the existing difficulties and the only adequate means of their removal. If this be so, there *can* be *no* question before the people half so momentous as this. *Shall we have men in power who will carry out these principles!* At different times, other great questions have claimed pre-eminence. There are other questions now before the people ; but I maintain that the question of *Slave Extension* towers immeasurably above them all. This is something more than a so-called "political" ques-. tion. It is interlinked with the most sacred interests of our holy religion. Is it nothing to the cause of Christianity whether the wide and glorious territory now the matter of dispute, be doomed to Slavery or not ? Whether a full and free gospel, for the entire population, shall, or shall not, be preached in that territory ? Whether the type of Christianity and of Christian churches there to be planted, be that of the free or of the Slave States ? Is *Religion* no way concerned in all this ?

And then, again, I ask, if Christianity, the world over, is not interested in the question of the peace and perpetuity of this Republic ? I do firmly believe that the arrest of slave extension is *essential* to the well-being of the *South*, as well as of the North—of the *whole country*. This the only way of preserving the Union. Unless it be arrested, I cannot see how a fatal rupture is to be avoided.*

He who aims to check the usurpations of the Slave Power, is, therefore, the true friend of his country. Much is said of *conservatism*. A *true* conservative every man ought to be. But there is a *false* conservatism which is exceedingly popular, as there is also an eliminated gospel which ignores the great doctrines of universal divine authority and human brotherhood. *Indifference* is not conservatism. Much less is that doctrine worthy of this name, which teaches the duty of quiet submission to the rapid encroachments of a rising

---

* The following from a distinguished Judge of the Supreme Court of the United States, (Judge McLEAN,) has appeared since this discourse was delivered : "No intelligent observer can fail to see that the tendency of our institutions is now rapidly downward, and all history and experience show that no free government, with such tendencies, was ever arrested in its declining career, without a revolution, either by a peaceful change of its policy and rulers, or by the bloody arbitrament of the sword."

What is it but the prevailing opinion of the most sober and thoughtful minds ? Says Dr. FRANCIS WAYLAND, late President of Brown University :—"It is the most solemn crisis the country has seen since we became a nation. On the decision of the passing season depend results of good or evil for the remotest prosperity. The interests of republican liberty, the world over, are in the balance."

The Hon. JOSIAH QUINCY, Sen., but utters a common sentiment :—"If we do not act now, the chance may never again return ; and all that will be left the North will be to tackle in with the slaves, and drag the carts of slaveholders, only beseeching them to spare the whip and make the load as light as possible."

despotism. Peace does not lie in this direction. Will the free men of the North ever submit to have slavery nationalized, and liberty, as applied to this glorious land, a by-word among the nations? *Ought* they to submit? Who that has a spark of the martyr spirit of our forefathers would not shrink from the avowal of such a sentiment? Is that conservatism, then, which hushes into silence all outspoken remonstrance, through fear of " excitement," and preaches " peace" as a condition of safety? If a band of invaders were burning down your city, would they be the true conservatists who should counsel quiet inaction and delay?

As long as slave usurpation continues, there can be no peace. This line of policy is the direct road to inevitable ruin. Certainly not until *this* generation of men dies out, will slavery be permitted to drag her slimy folds over these fair portions of our domain, where now Freedom smiles, and beckons the nations to emulate her example in the career of moral and physical elevation.

He, then, who at this moment speaks and acts in behalf of free principles, and he alone, is the *true* conservative. He, alone, is the *consistent* friend of the *whole country*. He has at heart, not the good of a *section* or a part of the Union, but aims to keep sound and entire the *whole body politic*, by restoring the original policy, and removing the *causes* which tend to a disastrous rupture.

In this noble endeavor, I again say, let there be unanimity of action. Let not effort be lost from misdirection. Let it *now* be aimed to compass the ends here indicated. Other points may be met as they shall assume paramount importance. Never was concerted action more imperatively demanded than at *this very moment*. We are, so to speak, compelled to forget minor differences, and strike hands together, as did our fathers, in the defence of Freedom. The question to be decided is, shall the lovers of liberty now stand in solid phalanx for its protection, or shall it be taken captive, and made, "with its sightless eyes, to grind in its prison-house forever?"

In settling this question, and settling it once for all, party predilictions and prejudices ought to sink into oblivion. The Slave Power is united ; why should those opposed to its encroachments be divided? A few years, it may be one year—aye, less than this—must determine the vast affairs to which I have alluded. The boast of a chief leader of the ruffian horde, just borne to us is, " *In a few months, in my opinion, there will not be an abolitionist left in Kansas ; they will be swept with a clean broom. Then the war will be carried elsewhere, if war we are to have.*" Aye, " *then,*" if need

be, "the war will be carried *elsewhere!* Let it be pondered well !
In this hour of the country's peril, therefore, let the lovers of Freedom stand side by side, and all is gained ; otherwise, there is reason for fear that all will be lost.

O ! shall it be, when the blood of an unoffending brother is spilt in the very palladium of our liberties ; when the Capitol is changed into the arena of personal violence ; when law makers are the perpetrators of the blackest crimes ; when plantation discipline is being brought to bear to transform freemen of the North into white serfs of southern nobility; when upon soil once sacredly devoted to freedom, the blood of peaceable and liberty-loving men is being wickedly shed with Executive authority and pretended judicial forms ; when a cruel despotism is bent on forcing upon that territory the foulest blot and deadliest scourge that fallen humanity ever suffered ; and when, under the agitation of this diabolical outrage, the very foundations of the Republic are heaving and quivering on their pivot, and foreign despots, as they look upon its threatened doom, are tossing their heads and crying out, Aha ! Aha ! so would we have it !—at *such* a time—at such a *fearful crisis—shall* it be that party names, and party prejudices, and personal preferences, shall keep apart those who ought to grasp each other's hands, and, by God's help, hold up the trembling pillars of the National fabric !

The Lord turn the heart of each man to his fellow ! The Lord make you a unit ! The Lord bring to nought the devices of wicked and ambitious men ! The Lord send relief to the wronged and oppressed ! The Lord give us men after his own heart ! The Lord save this Commonwealth, and still make it a name and a praise throughout the earth !

THE RESPONSIBILITY OF CHRISTIAN CITIZENSHIP,

The following timely words, condensed from a leading religious journal, are appended to fill out the otherwise two blank pages :

Christians sometimes excuse themselves from going to the polls and from taking any active interest in politics, on the plea that a few votes more or less cannot materially affect the result of an election, and therefore, since they can do no good by voting, they choose to avoid the excitements of a political campaign. Let us look at this plea. Does the fact that we cannot be sure of accomplishing a great and manifest good, lessen our obligation to use all reasonable effort for that end? Shall Christians reason thus, because in a given community they chance to be in a minority, or because they are but a very small minority of the population of the globe? The ability and the opportunity to act, and not the estimated results of action, are the measure of Christian obligation. But the possible results of our action may also come in to enhance that obligation. The *may be* often gives additional emphasis to the *ought*. We must obey the dictates of conscience, the sense of right, the calls of humanity and of Providence, even when we cannot see the promise of immediate good : but when to the plain dictates of Conscience, Humanity, and Religion are added, even the possible results of good from our action or evil from our inaction, the obligation to "do with our might that which our hand findeth to do" becomes more urgent and impressive.

Now nothing can be more illusive than this very plea that a single vote will accomplish nothing for the good of the country, nothing to secure just counsels, nothing to hinder the triumph of deceit and oppression, because it is but one. There have been crises memorable in history, both in the British Parliament and in the early Colonial legislation in this country, when measures portentous with the destiny of nations and of ages hung upon a single vote. And under our popular form of government, a single vote is likely at any time to determine the election of public officers, or in legislative bodies to settle measures of momentous interest to a State or to the Nation. Twice, within recent date, was a Governor of the State of Massachusetts elected by one vote. In one instance a single vote gave him a majority in the popular election. In the other he was elected by a majority of one, in the Legislature, in default of election by the people. By how small a majority was Mr. Banks chosen Speaker of the House of Representatives. And yet how much of the efficiency of the present Congress in behalf of Constitutional freedom is due to the two or three votes that placed him in the Speaker's chair. The other day the vote to admit Kansas as a Free State under the Topeka Constitution, was *lost by one vote*, after every preliminary measure had been carried. Again, the motion to reconsider that fatal resolve was carried by two votes, and then the bill to recognize freedom in Kansas prevailed by only two votes. One single vote may infold within itself blessings or miseries that future generations alone can estimate.

To apply this to the case in hand. The following is the apportionment of Presidential electors in the Free and Slave States respectively :

SIXTEEN FREE STATES.		FIFTEEN SLAVE STATES.	
Maine	8	Delaware	3
New Hampshire	5	Maryland	8
Vermont	5	Virginia	15
Massachusetts	13	North Carolina	10
Rhode Island	4	South Carolina	8
Connecticut	6	Georgia	10
New York	35	Florida	3
New Jersey	7	Alabama	9
Pennsylvania	27	Mississirpi	7
Ohio	28	Louisiana	6
Indiana	13	Texas	4
Illinois	11	Tennessee	12
Michigan	6	Kentucky	12
Wisconsin	5	Missouri	9
California	4	Arkansas	4
Total	176	Total	120
Grand Total	296	Necessary to choice	149

The South must be taken as a unit for the extension of slavery. The addition of Pennsylvania to the Southern vote would swell that vote to 147, lacking only two of a majority. Therefore every other Free State must be carried by the friends of freedom, if Pennsylvania shall join her strength to the sale oligarchy. The vote of any one State in the other direction, would, in that case, turn the scale in favor of sectional despotism against Constitutional freedom.

A plurality of votes in any of the Free States, carries the *whole number of Electors for that State.* ONE VOTE may therefore determine the choice of any one State, and *that State may turn the scale of the Union.* Yet thousands neglect going to the polls because they have only *one vote.* At the Presidential election of 1852, in New Jersey, of 119,557 adult males, only 83,211 voted. Where were the 36,000? Evidently thousands and tens of thousands who are entitled to vote, do not vote at all. · These are probably quiet, retiring citizens, who, if they should vote at all, would be likely to vote on the right side.

Are you, reader, of this number? Look, we pray you, at what God now requires of you as a citizen. You can see that the Emperor Alexander, as the ruler of 62,000,000 of people, and the proprietor of 23,000,000 of serfs, whose destinies he can control by a word, has a direct and fearful responsibility to God for the use of that power. But unless the whole theory of popular sovereignty is a sham, the power deposited in your hands as a voter may determine interests as momentous as lie within the will of the Emperor of Russia. *Your* vote may decide whether this fair land shall be filled with the fruits of Christian civilization or with the bitter and deadly fruits of slavery. Who can be indifferent to such a responsibility?